CHIHUA... (LONGHAIRED) OWNERS GUIDE

The Best Guide On The Care, Raising, Feeding, Socializing, Breeding, Exercise, Health, Cost, Complete Management And Loving Your Dog

DR. OKUS OSCAR

Contents

CHAPTER ONE

Chihuahua (Longhaired)

Your dog is one of a kind! She is your most trusted confidante, constant companion, and a wellspring of affection that is never conditional. You probably picked her because you adore Chihuahuas, and you probably expected her to have specific qualities that would make her suitable for your way of life, such as the following:

• Aware, inquisitive, and busy

• Capable of adjusting to a wide range of environmental situations

• Self-assured and able to fend for themselves;

• A watchdog who is always alert and ready to bark

• Doesn't require a lot of activity

• Only needs a little bit of grooming

On the other hand, no dog is perfect. It's possible that you've also observed the following characteristics:

• Can be fearful, aggressive, or snappy if not properly socialized

- Requires early socialization to tolerate other dogs and strangers

- Due to her small size, she is fragile and easily hurt

- Requires continuous attention from her family

- Brave and courageous, they have been known to assault considerably larger canines

- They have a propensity for barking an excessive amount

Is It All Worthwhile In The End?

Of course! She has a lot of character, which is one of the reasons you like her so much. She is a devoted and watchful member of the family who requires constant attention from everyone. Because of her diminutive size, she is an ideal companion while traveling.

There are two types of Chihuahua coats: smooth and longhaired. This kind of dog is the tiniest of all the breeds of canines. They are recognized for their enormous, upright ears and conspicuous large eyes and their origin can be traced back to Mexico where they were raised for companionship. The temperament of a Chihuahua is similar to that of a terrier in that she is brave and dedicated to her family and friends. The Chihuahua is a breed of dog that, on average, lives between 12 and 14 years. They are known for their robust health. They are known to be affected by various disorders that are rather frequent, such as luxating patella and cataracts. Be sure to schedule routine exams for yourself because early detection is the key to living a long and happy life.

The Condition Of Your Chihuahua With A Long Coat

We are aware that you feel an immense amount of responsibility for your dog, and as a result, you want to provide the best possible care for her. Because of this, we have compiled a summary of the health problems that we will be going over with you during the course of your Chihuahua's life. If we are aware of the health issues that are unique to Longhaired Chihuahuas, we will be able to create a preventative health plan that will help us monitor for and maybe avoid some of the dangers that are predicted.

There are a number of diseases and problems that are genetic, which means they are tied to the breed of your pet. The researchers who study canine genetics and the veterinarians who practice them have come to the conclusion that the diseases we've mentioned in this article have a considerable rate of occurrence and/or influence in this breed of dog. That does not mean that these issues will manifest themselves in your dog; rather, it indicates that she is at a greater risk than other dogs. In order to give you an idea of what may arise in the future with your Longhaired Chihuahua, we are going to outline the most typical problems associated with these dogs. Naturally, we are unable to cover every possibilities in this article; thus, make sure to get in touch with us if you observe any peculiar indications or symptoms.

This book discusses the most significant genetic predispositions that are associated with Longhaired Chihuahuas as well as general health information that is relevant to all dogs. Having this information allows you and us to collaborate on a plan to meet the one-of-a-kind medical requirements of your pet. We have also included, at the very end of the pamphlet, a summary of what you may do while at home to maintain the health and appearance of your Chi in the best possible way. You will be aware of what to look out for, and the knowledge that we are providing your friend with the highest level of care will make all of us feel better.

CHAPTER TWO

Information Concerning The General Health Of Your Long-Haired Chihuahua

Diseases Of The Teeth

Dental disease is the most frequent form of chronic illness that can be seen in pets; by the age of two, it affects eighty percent of all dogs.

Your Longhaired Chihuahua is, regrettably, more likely than other breeds of dog to have issues with her teeth. The formation of tartar on the teeth is the initial step, followed by infection of the gums and the tooth roots as the condition worsens. Your friend will lose her teeth and be at risk of experiencing damage to her kidneys, liver, heart, and joints if we do not take measures to prevent or cure dental disease on her behalf.

In point of fact, the lifespan of your Longhaired Chihuahua could be reduced by anything from one to three years! We'll give your dog's teeth a professional cleaning on a regular basis and advise you on what you can do to maintain their gleaming whiteness at home.

Infections

Chihuahuas with long hair are prone to bacterial and viral infections, including parvovirus, rabies, and distemper, the same kinds of illnesses that can affect other breeds of dogs. We will prescribe vaccination for her since it is the best way to protect her against the diseases that are prevalent in our area, as well as her age and other considerations. Many of these infections are preventable.

Obesity

Longhaired Chihuahuas are susceptible to developing a number of serious health issues, one of which is obesity. It is a dangerous condition that has the potential to cause or worsen back pain, metabolic and digestive difficulties, joint problems, and heart disease. You can "love her to death" with any leftover food from people meals as well as doggy goodies, despite the fact that it is tempting to offer your friend food when she looks at you with those soulful eyes. Instead, you should give her a cuddle, brush her fur or teeth, play a game with her, or maybe even take her on a walk. She'll appreciate it. You will feel better after she does, and so will she!

Parasites

Both the inside and the outside of your Chi's body can be colonized by a wide variety of parasitic worms and insects. Her skin and ears are susceptible to infestation from a wide variety of parasites, including fleas, ticks, and ear mites. It is possible for her body to become infected with hookworms, roundworms, heartworms, and whipworms through a variety of means, including ingesting contaminated water, walking barefoot on polluted soil, or being bitten by an infected mosquito. Some of these parasites have the potential to be passed on to you or a member of your family, making them a significant cause for concern for everyone. It is critical that we perform regular checks for the presence of these parasites because they can cause your canine companion pain, discomfort, and even death. Therefore, it is necessary that we perform these checks. In addition, we will offer recommendations for preventative medication that may be required to keep her healthy.

Castration Or Sterilization (S/N)

Having your Chihuahua spayed is one of the most beneficial things you can do for her, and she will thank you for it (neutered for males). When performing this procedure on a female patient, the ovaries and the uterus are surgically removed.

When performing this procedure on a male patient, the testicles are surgically removed. The risk of developing some forms of cancer is reduced when a pet is spayed or neutered, and you no longer have to worry about your animal producing litters of pups or kittens that you don't want.

While your pet is under anesthesia for this procedure, we will be able to diagnose and treat some of the ailments that your dog is likely to develop in the future. This offers us the opportunity to better care for your dog. For instance, if your pet requires hip X-rays or if a puppy tooth has to be pulled, now would be an excellent time to schedule such procedures.

This is a simple solution for both you and your friend, which is convenient. Testing the patient's blood on a routine basis before to surgery enables us to recognize common issues that raise the risk of anesthesia or operation and to take appropriate preventative measures.

Don't worry; when the time comes, we'll talk about the particular issues that we'll be looking for and how to spot them.

CHAPTER THREE

Problems With The Eyesight Of Long-Haired Chihuahuas That Can Be Caused By Genetics

There aren't many things that can have as significant of an effect on the quality of life of your dog as ensuring that his eyes are healthy and functioning properly. Unfortunately, Longhaired Chihuahuas have a higher risk of inheriting or developing a number of different eye conditions than other Chihuahua breeds.

Some of these conditions, if left untreated for an extended period of time, can lead to blindness, and the majority of these conditions can cause excruciating pain. At each exam, we will check his eyes to see if there are any warning signals that could cause worry.

Glaucoma, an eye illness that can affect humans as well as Longhaired Chihuahuas, is a disease that causes excruciating pain and, if it is not treated, swiftly progresses to the point where it causes blindness.

 Squinting, watery eyes, bluing of the cornea (the transparent front part of the eye), and redness in the whites of the eyes are some of the symptoms that come along with dry eye syndrome. Pain is frequently present, but owners of pets very seldom perceive it, despite the fact that it can be rather severe.

People who experience specific varieties of glaucoma frequently describe the sensation as being similar to that of having an ice pick thrust into their eye.

Yikes! In more severe cases, the eye may appear enlarged or swollen, giving the impression that it is bulging outward. We will conduct his annual glaucoma screening in order to diagnose him as soon as possible and get him started on therapy. Glaucoma is a condition that must be treated immediately. If you see any symptoms, don't hesitate to give us a call; instead, head to the nearest emergency room.

Dry eye, sometimes referred to as keratoconjunctivitis sicca or KCS, is a condition that frequently affects Longhaired Chihuahuas. Because the glands that create tears are unable to produce enough tears to keep the eye moist, the eye becomes inflamed, irritated, and susceptible to infection. Ouch! Some of the symptoms include a heavy discharge, squinting, pawing at the eye, or the look of an eye that is dull and dry. It is important that you get in touch with us as soon as possible if you have any of these symptoms because this ailment is quite uncomfortable. When we examine him, we are going to check his tear production. If he does have this ailment, we will write you a prescription for an ointment that you will need to apply to your dog for the rest of its life.

In senior Chihuahuas, cataracts are a leading cause of irreversible vision loss. When we check him, we will be on the lookout for the lenses in his eyes to grow more opaque, which means that they will appear foggy rather than clear. Despite their eyesight loss, many dogs are able to adapt positively and have normal lives. There is also the possibility of undergoing surgery to have cataracts surgically removed and one's vision restored.

CHAPTER FOUR

Coronary Artery Disease

When Longhaired Chihuahuas reach their senior years, heart failure is the most common cause of mortality that they experience. The majority of cases of canine heart disease are brought on by a valve that has become weak.

One of the heart's valves steadily deteriorates to the point where it can no longer close completely. The subsequent backflow of blood around this valve causes the heart to work harder than it should. A heart murmur is present in animals that suffer from heart valve disease, which is also referred to as mitral valve disease. We will undertake tests to establish the degree of the condition in your dog if he or she has a heart murmur or other outward indicators suggesting that there may be a problem with the heart.

In order to keep an eye on the issue, the previous tests will need to be redone at least once per year. If the condition of his heart valves is caught in its early stages, we may be able to treat him with medications that will add many years to his life expectancy. Dental care from a veterinarian, as well as the replenishment of fatty acids, can help prevent heart disease, and maintaining a healthy weight can help reduce the severity of its symptoms.

Chihuahuas have an increased risk of developing a problem known as patent ductus arteriosis, which occurs when a tiny channel that should stop shortly after birth but instead continues to carry blood between two sections of the heart does not do so. This causes an excessive amount of blood to be delivered to the lungs, which leads to fluid retention and strain on the heart. The symptoms that are visible to others can be rather subtle, or they can be more severe and include coughing, exhaustion during exercise, weight loss, shortness of breath, or weakness in the rear limbs. In order to diagnose this issue during the course of his examinations, we will be listening for a certain form of cardiac murmur. If your friend suffers from this issue, we might suggest that they have surgery to have the troublesome vessel closed down.

Knee Problems

It's possible that the kneecap (patella) of your Chihuahua will dislocate on occasion (called patellar luxation). It's possible that you'll observe that as he runs along, he occasionally kicks up one foot behind him and skips or hops for a few steps.

Then, he pops his kneecap back into position by kicking his leg out to the side, and everything is normal after that. If the issue is not severe and affects only one leg, your friend may not need much treatment other than arthritis medicine. When the symptoms are severe, surgery may be required to realign the kneecap and prevent it from popping out of position. This can be done to prevent further kneecap dislocation.

Collapse Of The Trachea

The trachea, often known as the windpipe, is composed of rings of cartilage, giving it an appearance similar to that of the ridged hose of a vacuum cleaner. This structure, like the hose, possesses both flexibility and strength in equal measure. There is a possibility that the cartilage rings in Longhaired Chihuahuas will be fragile or will have formed improperly. It is possible for the trachea to collapse and become overly narrow, which will result in coughing and make it difficult to breathe. The majority of occurrences of tracheal collapse are moderate, and medicine is used to alleviate the symptoms of the condition. Surgery is a possibility to consider when the symptoms are severe.

Necrosis Of The Hip

The painful degenerative hip ailment known as Legg-Calve-Perthes Disease is more likely to affect young Longhaired Chihuahuas than other breeds. It is still not totally understood what causes this ailment, although it is assumed to be an issue with the blood flow to the hip, which causes the femoral head (the top of the thigh bone) to become brittle and readily fracture. The specific etiology of this condition is still not completely understood. Ouch! This condition, which typically manifests itself between the ages of six and nine months, can cause pain and lameness in either or both of the animal's hind legs, and it frequently necessitates surgical intervention.

CHAPTER FIVE

Bleeding Disorders

Hemophilia is a condition that can affect your Longhaired Chihuahua and other breeds of Chihuahua. Before we proceed with the operation, we are going to check his blood clotting time by performing diagnostic testing.

Because we may not discover that your pet has this illness until major bleeding occurs during surgery or after a traumatic injury, this test is very crucial.

Liver Problems

Your Chi is more likely than other dogs to suffer from a condition known as portosystemic shunt, which affects the liver (PSS). Because a portion of the blood supply that ought to go to the liver instead flows around it, the liver is deprived of the blood flow that is necessary for it to develop and operate appropriately.

In the event that your friend has PSS, his liver will be unable to properly eliminate poisons from his bloodstream. Every time he gets anesthesia, we will evaluate his liver function in addition to performing a routine preanesthetic panel so that we can make sure that he does not have this condition. In the event that he develops symptoms like slowed growth or seizures, we will test his blood and perhaps perform an ultrasound check of his liver. It's possible that surgery will be required, but in certain instances, we can treat the condition with a specialized diet and some medications.

Bladder Or Kidney Stones

There are several distinct kinds of stones that can develop in either the kidney or the bladder, and Longhaired Chihuahuas have an increased risk of developing these stones in comparison to other breeds of dogs. We will periodically analyze his urine to look for telltale indicators that indicate the existence of painful kidney and bladder stones; these stones can cause a lot of discomfort. Urgent medical attention is required if your friend is unable to urinate, has blood in his urine, or is in pain when trying to urinate. Make contact with us right away!

Reproductive Difficulties

Breeds that have a large head in comparison to their pelvis size are more likely to experience complications during the birthing process. Her pelvis is simply not big enough to accommodate the passage of puppies, thus a C-section is frequently necessary to ensure both her health and the health of her offspring. Talk to us beforehand if you want to breed your Chi, if that's something you're interesting in doing. We are here to assist you in making an educated decision that takes into account the body conformation of both the sire and the dam.

Retained Teeth From A Puppy

Around the age of four months, canines typically start to lose their primary teeth (also known as their "puppy" teeth). It's possible for the permanent teeth to become infected or damaged if the baby teeth don't fall out when they're supposed to, right as the adult teeth are emerging. Small dog breeds, such as Chihuahuas, seem to have a higher incidence of retained teeth. Food and hair become lodged in the gap between the main tooth and the regular adult tooth because of the retained puppy teeth. If neglected, the condition can lead to painful gums, foul breath, and even the loss of adult teeth. We will keep an eye on his teeth as they continue to develop and may suggest extraction of his puppy teeth if they are present alongside his adult teeth.

Neurologic Problems

Longhaired Chihuahuas are susceptible to a number of different neurologic illnesses. Seizures, unsteadiness, tremors, weakness, or excessive sleeping are some of the symptoms that may be associated with neurological issues. If you observe any of these signs, it is imperative that you seek veterinarian assistance as soon as possible.

CHAPTER SIX

Low Blood Sugar

Hypoglycemia, which is often referred to as low blood sugar, is a problem that is rather common in young dogs of tiny breeds, including Longhaired Chihuahuas. There are a variety of situations that could bring it on. Weakness, collapse, and seizures are some of the physical indications that might be seen. These symptoms could appear after a vigorous workout, a very exciting event, or even after going without food for a while. Please get in touch with us as soon as possible if your child exhibits any of these symptoms. Fortunately, most people are able to outgrow this illness once they begin receiving treatment at such an early age.

Allergies

When a person has an allergy to pollen, mold, or dust, they will experience symptoms such as sneezing and itchy eyes. Dogs do not sneeze when they have allergies; rather, their skin becomes itchy. This type of skin allergy is referred to as "atopy," and Chihuahuas are frequently affected by it. In most cases, the areas most susceptible to infection include the feet, abdomen, folds of the skin, and ears. The onset of symptoms normally occurs between the ages of one and three, and they may become more severe with each passing year. The most typical symptoms include licking and rubbing the face and paws, as well as having frequent ear infections. The good news is that this ailment may be treated in a variety of ways, and there are numerous solutions available.

Injuries To The Spinal Cord

When compared to other breeds of dogs, Longhaired Chihuahuas have a higher risk of developing instability in the first two neck vertebrae (called the atlantal and the axial vertebrae). This can result in an abrupt injury to the spinal cord in the neck area. It is likely that your dog is in discomfort if he suddenly becomes unable or unwilling to leap up or go up stairs, screams for no apparent reason, or attempts to turn or lower his head when you pick him up. Make contact with us right away! We will try to control the discomfort with medicines, but there are situations when surgery is the best option. Losing weight and keeping it off can help stave off obesity-related ailments, like so many others. It is imperative that you start using ramps or steps for your dog as soon as he is a puppy if you have a dog of this breed so that he does not spend his entire life putting strain on his neck by jumping on and off of the furniture.

Mange

Demodex is a type of mite that is extremely small and lives in the hair follicles of dogs. They are present in every dog. Some dog breeds, like your Chihuahua, are predisposed to have an excessive amount of these mites on their fur, despite the fact that the immune system of a dog normally serves to keep the mite population under control. In circumstances where the condition is not severe, pet owners could discover a few lesions that are bald, dry, and irritating. It's common for them to show up on the face or feet, and they might or might not be itchy. There is a possibility of secondary skin infections. It is critical to seek veterinary care as soon as possible in order to stop the spread of the disease. While the majority of pets appear to outgrow the issue over time, others have to be managed throughout their entire lives.

The Effect Of Water On The Brain

Hydrocephalus is a condition that develops when fluid accumulates inside the skull and causes pressure to be exerted on the brain. This issue is more frequent in breeds that have dome-shaped heads, such as your Longhaired Chihuahua, which is why it is so easy to spot in your dog. It frequently occurs when the bones of the skull fail to fuse together in the correct manner. Seizures, trouble housebreaking the puppy, diminished mental function, circling, and a spastic gait are all indicators of this condition. In most cases, the disease is identified at a young age, although we do have cases where adult dogs have been affected. During her appointments, we will keep this risk in mind and encourage early testing as well as discuss several choices for effective treatment in the event that symptoms occur.

CHAPTER SEVEN

Providing At-Home Veterinarian Care For Your Long-Haired Chihuahua

The majority of what you can do to ensure the happiness and wellbeing of your dog can be summed up in a single word: common sense.

Keep an eye on her diet, make sure she gets plenty of exercise, brush her teeth and coat on a regular basis, and contact us or a pet emergency hospital if something appears out of the ordinary (for a list of things to look out for, see "What to Watch For" below). Be sure to stick to the schedule of checkups and vaccines that we have outlined for her. It is in her best interest.

This is the time when we will perform the required "check-ups" on her and look for signs of diseases and conditions that are typical of Chihuahuas. Signing up for pet health insurance is another extremely crucial step in providing proper care for your animal companion. There is a good chance that she will require various medical tests and operations throughout the course of her life, and having pet health insurance will assist you in meeting the financial obligations associated with these needs.

Care Routines, Diet, And Physical Activity

Include her regular care in your schedule so that you may help your Chi enjoy a longer, healthier, and happier life over the course of her entire lifetime. It is impossible to place enough emphasis on maintaining a healthy diet and regular exercise routine.

• Take the same precautions with your pet that you would with a young child. Maintain a closed door policy, be sure to pick up after yourself, and section off rooms as required. She won't be able to get into mischief and she won't be able to access things that she shouldn't put in her mouth because of this.

• Brush her coat as needed, at least weekly to prevent mats. \s• Longhaired Chihuahuas normally have good teeth, and you can keep them perfect by brushing them at least twice a week!

Even when she was a puppy, you should clean her ears once a week. Don't be concerned; we'll walk you through it!

• Extremely susceptible to the cold, making it imperative to wear warm clothing during the winter months.

• She will need a daily walk and regular inside play; she is well-suited for apartment living. • Due to her forceful temperament and small size, she is not advised for homes with young children.

• Maintain a set diet for your dog, and under no circumstances should you feed her table scraps.

• Ensure that she consumes a food of high nutritional value that is suitable for her age.

• Make sure your dog gets enough of exercise on a regular basis, but don't push him too hard at first.

What To Look Out For

Any aberrant symptom could be an indication of a dangerous sickness, or it could just be a minor or temporary condition. It is important to keep an open mind about this. It is essential to have the ability to determine when it is necessary to seek veterinarian assistance and the degree of urgency involved. Your Longhaired Chihuahua may be suffering from one of the many diseases that cause dogs to exhibit a distinctive pattern of symptoms.

These symptoms, when taken together, may serve as an obvious warning that your dog requires medical attention.

Printed in Great Britain
by Amazon

27132524R00036